Armistice
1918

Reg Grant

W
HODDER
Wayland

An imprint of Hodder Children's Books

THE WORLD WARS

© 2000 White-Thomson Publishing Ltd

Produced for Hodder Wayland by
White-Thomson Publishing Ltd
2/3 St. Andrew's Place
Lewes
BN7 1UP

Series concept: Alex Woolf
Editor: Jonathan Ingoldby
Designer: Simon Borrough
Consultant: Malcolm Brown

A catalogue record for this book is available from the British
Library.

ISBN 0 7502 2636 6

Printed and bound in Italy by G. Canale & CSpa., Turin

Hodder Children's Books
A division of Hodder Headline plc
338 Euston Road, London NW1 3BH

Cover photographs: Hodder Wayland Picture Library

Picture acknowledgements
AKG London 25 (bottom), 55
(bottom); Hodder Wayland Picture
Library 5, 7, 10, 12, 13, 22, 29; The
Hulton Getty Picture Collection 9,
48, 57; Peter Newark's Military
Pictures 4, 6, 8, 14, 16, 17, 18, 19,
21, 26, 27, 30, 32, 33, 34–5, 37,
39, 40, 41, 42, 46, 47 (top), 49
(bottom), 50, 51, 52, 53, 54;
Popperfoto 11, 20, 23, 24, 25, 28
(top), 36, 44, 45, 47 (bottom), 49
(top), 55 (top) 56, 58, 59.

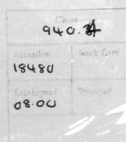

Contents

A Great War ends

In the early hours of the morning of 11 November 1918, a small group of men stepped down from a railway carriage in a siding at Rethondes in the Forest of Compiègne in eastern France. They were a delegation of German officials and officers headed by the respected moderate politician Matthias Erzberger. In the darkness, they filed on planks across wet muddy ground to a parallel track where another carriage was drawn up in the forest. This was the command train of Marshal Ferdinand Foch, the commander-in-chief of the Allied armies in France. The Germans were about to concede that the most destructive war in history up to that time – a conflict now known as World War I, but then simply referred to as 'the Great War' – was over.

11 November 1918: Marshal Foch, second from right, is photographed with the Allied delegation outside the railway carriage in which the armistice was signed.

World at war

Along a line stretching from Belgium in the north to the Swiss border in the south, many thousands of soldiers confronted one another in armed conflict, as they had done since the early months of the war in 1914. Initially, Germany and Austria-Hungary – the Central Powers – had fought Britain, France, Russia, Belgium and Serbia – the Allies. Over the following four years, the war had broadened into a global conflict. Although Russia had dropped out, Bulgaria and the Turkish Ottoman Empire had come in on Germany's side, while many other countries, including Italy, Romania and the United States had joined the war in support of the Allies. More than 8 million soldiers had lost their lives in the titanic struggle. Battle was still raging in many sectors of the front. British Empire, French, US and Belgian troops pressed forward toward the German border, liberating territory that had been under German occupation for four years.

Canadian troops advance eastward across France, pursuing the retreating Germans in the autumn of 1918.

Signing the armistice

Erzberger and his colleagues were in a grim mood. They had been instructed by the German government and military authorities in Berlin to accept an armistice – an agreement to end the fighting. The armistice terms had been laid down by their enemies, and seemed harsh to the Germans. Confronting Foch inside his railway carriage, Erzberger made a statement protesting against the terms imposed on Germany. He ended: 'A people of seventy million are suffering, but they are not dead.' However, Foch was unyielding; he was not there to negotiate terms, but to impose them. Just after 5 a.m., Erzberger and other delegation members signed the armistice agreement.

An artist's impression of the scene inside Foch's railway carriage: the leader of the German delegation, Matthias Erzberger, confronts Marshal Foch across the table on which the armistice will be signed.

An order went out to the forces under Foch's command: 'Hostilities will cease at 11 a.m. today. Defensive precautions will be maintained.' Some commanders ordered attacks that morning to seize bridges or high points before the armistice came into effect. At Mons, Belgium, three British soldiers who had fought through the entire four years of the war were killed by machine-gun fire on the last morning. The timing of the ceasefire had been deliberately chosen to be memorable: the eleventh hour of the eleventh day of the eleventh month of 1918. Along the battle lines and amid the shattered ruins of towns and villages, the guns fell silent.

Celebration and mourning

There was curiously little rejoicing among the troops on the victorious side. Most took the news quietly and, as ordered, simply stayed at their posts. In the cities of Britain, France and the United States, however, there were scenes of unbridled jubilation. French Prime Minister Georges Clemenceau was hailed by cheering crowds, emerging onto the balcony of his Paris house to acknowledge the applause. In London, work stopped for the day once the news broke. Crowds of servicemen on leave and joyful civilians packed Trafalgar Square and even lit a bonfire at the base of Nelson's Column. It was the same story on Broadway in New York and in other North American cities.

After the guns have fallen silent, a US soldier writes a letter in the ruins of a village. Many soldiers wrote home immediately after the armistice to let their families know that they had survived.

On Armistice Day, French Prime Minister Georges Clemenceau commented privately:

'We have won the war. Now we will have to win the peace. That may prove harder.'

Source: A. Palmer, *Victory 1918*

The scenes of rejoicing around Trafalgar Square, London, on Armistice Day were wild and riotous. Soldiers took the lead, relieved that they would not now be sent to die in battle.

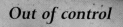

Out of control

Across the world, as news of the armistice spread, celebrating crowds took to the streets in demonstrations of joy that often verged on riots. In Chicago, USA, according to one newspaper report, some people 'wore inverted waste baskets over their heads to protect their hats from the sticks and stones of men and women revellers who lined the walls of buildings'. In the Australian city of Melbourne, crowds ran wildly out of control. One group of revellers took over a tramcar and crashed it through the front window of an office. Others looted Chinese-owned shops, stealing fireworks which were then let off in the streets, terrifying many passers-by. Many people objected strongly to this riotous response to the armistice. A British army officer, Lieutenant Ansell, wrote in his diary:

'Too many of the best have given their lives for this hour and it should be one of thanksgiving rather than tomfoolery.'

But not everyone was in a mood for celebration. Millions were mourning sons or brothers lost at the front. The feared telegrams announcing a death in action continued to be delivered to families. Many turned to religion in the moment of victory, packing churches to pray in thanksgiving or in memory of the lost.

Children in a poor district of London's East End are treated to a tea party in the street to celebrate the end of the war. Their patriotic parents have hung flags from the windows.

Grief on Armistice Day

Wilfred Owen, now remembered as one of the greatest poets of the war, was killed in action on 4 November 1918. In his home town of Shrewsbury, England, the news of the armistice on 11 November was greeted by the prolonged ringing of church bells. Through the clamour of celebration, Owen's parents, Tom and Susan, heard the gentler chime of their front door bell. It was a messenger with an official telegram informing them of their son's death.

Wilfred Owen, wartime army officer and poet, who died a week before the armistice.

Bitter defeat

In much of the world, there was no cause for thanksgiving or rejoicing. The news of the armistice – a virtual surrender – shocked Germans, who had had no idea their army was on the verge of defeat. Berlin and Vienna, the capital cities of the defeated powers, were in the grip of revolutionary upheaval. Much of their population was suffering from severe food shortages, caused by a British naval blockade. Further east, in the former Russian Empire, conditions were far worse, as a new Bolshevik government, under Vladimir Ilyich Lenin, sought to impose its rule on a land shattered by war and revolution.

Austrian children collect firewood: for the defeated countries, the armistice brought bitterness and hardship.

Adolf Hitler, a corporal in the German army, was a patient in a hospital at Pasewalk, Pomerania, having been temporarily blinded by gas in the trenches, when he heard the news of the armistice. In his memoirs, *Mein Kampf*, he recalled the shock of that moment:

'*...everything went black before my eyes; I tottered and groped my way back to the dormitory, threw myself on my bunk, and dug my burning head into my blankets and pillow... so it had all been in vain...*'

Source: J. Fest, *Hitler*

The world was also in the grip of one of the most destructive epidemic diseases ever. Influenza of an especially virulent kind was killing thousands of people a week across the globe. This 'Spanish 'flu' would eventually cause the deaths of an estimated 12 million worldwide. At the moment when the armistice was announced, hundreds of thousands were seriously ill with this disease.

Uncertain future

With the end of the fighting, people's minds naturally turned to the future. How was a new world to be built on the ruins that the Great War had created? This book will explain how the armistice had come about, and what happened to the subsequent efforts to construct a peaceful and prosperous world.

In a speech to the House of Commons announcing the armistice, British prime minister David Lloyd George said:

'*Thus at eleven o'clock this morning came to an end the cruellest and most terrible war that has ever scourged mankind. I hope we may all say that thus, this fateful morning, came to an end all wars.*'

Source: M. Gilbert, *A History of the Twentieth Century Volume 1: 1900–1933*

The desolate spectacle of a road in Flanders at the end of the most destructive war that, until then, the world had ever seen.

Elusive peace

The major powers of Europe had stumbled into armed conflict in August 1914 with no clear aim apart from military victory itself. There was a widely-held belief that the war would be 'all over by Christmas'. The vast majority of people in the combatant countries supported the war. On both sides, they genuinely believed they were defending themselves against aggression and doing what was necessary for their national honour and security.

From the end of 1914, however, the war settled into a stalemate, and the prospect of victory for either side became remote. The cost of the war in human lives rose to unprecedented levels, as hundreds of thousands of soldiers died in unsuccessful attempts to break the enemy lines, which often resulted in huge losses in exchange for a few kilometres of muddy ground. Yet the leaders of the combatant countries were unable to find a basis for peace negotiations.

Stretcher-bearers knee-deep in mud during the 1917 battle of Passchendaele – a battle in which about 300,000 troops from Britain and its empire were killed or wounded for minimal gains.

Barriers to peace

It is far easier to start a war than to end it. Once massive efforts had been made, including a huge sacrifice of lives, people expected tangible gains to justify the death and hardship. They were reluctant to return to the situation before the war – the most obvious basis for a compromise peace – because it would make the sacrifice seem futile. Both sides saw it as a minimum requirement of peace that their enemies should be weakened, so they would be safe from a future attack. But it was logically impossible for both sides to achieve this objective at once.

The war also generated hatred. The British and French, for example, had denounced the Germans as barbarians because of atrocities committed in Belgium – which were real, even if exaggerated in Allied propaganda – and actions such as the sinking of the British ocean liner *Lusitania* by a U-boat in 1915. In Britain, popular hostility to all things German forced the royal family to change their name from Saxe-Coburg-Gotha to Windsor. Such attitudes made compromise difficult.

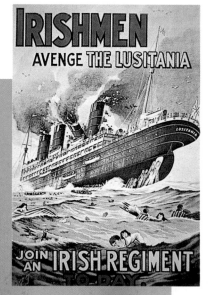

A poster using the sinking of the Lusitania *to encourage men to enlist and 'avenge' those who had died.*

The Lusitania riots

News of the sinking of the ocean liner *Lusitania* by a German submarine appeared in the British evening papers on 7 May 1915. Over 1,000 people were drowned in the disaster, 128 of them US citizens. Popular outrage swelled in Britain and the USA. In many British towns and cities over the following weekend, shops owned by Germans, or by people with German-sounding names, were attacked and looted. Workers demonstrated against being made to work alongside German employees in factories. The strength of popular feeling against Germany, shown by the *Lusitania* riots, helps explain why arguments for a compromise peace met with a hostile response from most British people throughout the war.

Secret ambitions

Each side gradually put together specific war aims as the conflict dragged on. Often written down in secret treaties, these aims made peace virtually impossible. The French, for example, not only wanted to recover the provinces of Alsace and Lorraine, which they had ceded to the Germans after their defeat in the Franco-Prussian War of 1871, but also to detach the Rhineland from Germany. This would be totally unacceptable to any German government. In order to bring Italy into the war on their side in 1915, Britain and France secretly agreed that the Italians could take territory from Austria-Hungary. This made peace with Austria-Hungary hard to achieve. Another secret treaty promised Russia control of Constantinople (Istanbul), the capital of Ottoman Turkey.

German ambitions also stood in the way of peace. German leaders were determined to keep the control of Belgium they had won at the start of the war. But Britain was totally committed to defending Belgian independence. Germany also wanted to maintain dominance in eastern Europe, where early victories had given it control of large areas of the Russian Empire. This ruled out a compromise peace with Russia.

Georges Clemenceau, an elderly but fiery radical, was appointed French prime minister in November 1917. Addressing the French Chamber of Deputies, he said:

'You ask what are my war aims. Gentlemen, they are very simple: Victory.'

Source: A.J.P. Taylor, *The First World War*

Peace without victory

One idealist believed that he could find a way to end the slaughter. This was Thomas Woodrow Wilson, the president of the neutral United States. Re-elected

New US recruits follow the band after the United States' entry into the war. The Americans had a very small peacetime army; it took a long time to train conscripts and transport them to the fighting in France.

president on a peace platform in November 1916, he put himself forward as a mediator between the warring powers, calling for 'peace without victory'. But the would-be peacemaker soon found himself leading the USA into the war. A combination of Germany's decision to launch unlimited U-boat warfare, including attacks on US ships bound for Britain, and the revelation of a foolish German plot to back a Mexican invasion of the United States, forced Wilson to declare war on Germany in April 1917.

Wilson was determined not to become a party to a cynical European power conflict. He announced that democracy was the fundamental cause for which the USA would fight: 'the world must be made safe for democracy'. He refused to become an ally of Britain and France, instead remaining an Associate Power with full independence of action. He presented himself as an advocate of a just peace and made a series of pronouncements refining his view of war aims, most notably in the 14-point plan of January 1918.

Woodrow Wilson

Born in Staunton, Virginia, in 1856, Thomas Woodrow Wilson was elected president of the United States in 1912, winning a second term four years later. Wilson was a high-minded university professor and lawyer who wanted to see political decisions based on moral ideals. He hated war and believed that democracy and progress could make it a thing of the past. Many who met him thought him cold and insufferably self-righteous, but in 1918 he was viewed by millions as their best hope for a future of peace and freedom.

On 8 January 1918, in a speech to Congress, Wilson announced a 14-point plan that he believed would provide the basis for a just and durable peace. There were to be no more secret deals between diplomats, but 'open covenants of peace openly arrived at'. Freedom of the seas and free trade were to be sacred. Arms cuts would be made 'to the lowest point consistent with domestic safety'. Germany would have to give back territory it had occupied during the war in Belgium, France and Russia, as well as Alsace-Lorraine, seized from France in 1871. Poland, which had been carved up between Russia, Prussias and Austria in the eighteenth century, would be restored as an independent state. Other national groups in the Austro-Hungarian and Ottoman Empires would have the right to 'the freest opportunity of autonomous development' – meaning they would not be independent, but would have a large say in running their own affairs. Finally, all countries would get together in an international organization that would guarantee the new borders, bringing 'international anarchy' to an end.

Wilson suffered a series of strokes during 1919 that left him physically and mentally incapacitated. He died in 1924.

President Woodrow Wilson appealed for the support of patriotic Americans, as he led them into a war that he said would make the world 'safe for democracy'.

War-weariness and revolution

By the time the United States entered the conflict in 1917, it looked as if the fighting might end through the war-weariness of ordinary people in Europe after years of slaughter. Popular disillusionment with the way governments were running the war and with the hardship it brought in its wake was widespread. In April 1917, mutiny swept through the French army. Over 100,000 men were court-martialled for refusing to obey orders. France's generals restored discipline, but knew that if they ordered an offensive their soldiers would probably refuse to fight. The Italian army practically ceased to fight after defeat at Caporetto in the autumn.

The Italian commander-in-chief Luigi Cadorna was sacked after Italy's disastrous defeat at Caporetto.

It was not only, or even primarily, in the front line that disillusionment spread. All the combatant countries had experienced sharp social conflicts before the war. In all of them there was a wide gap between rich and poor. Most had strong socialist movements that advocated the overthrow of the traditional ruling class. By 1917, many workers were convinced that wealthy profiteers were benefiting from a war for which ordinary people were paying with their lives. Strikes and food riots were widespread in Germany. Britain and France also experienced labour disputes and popular discontent.

Voices for peace

Nervously aware of the need to maintain the will to fight, combatant countries dealt harshly with those who spoke out against the war. In Germany, the independent socialist Karl Liebknecht was sentenced to four years hard labour for organizing anti-war protests. In the United States, the socialist Eugene Debs was sentenced to ten years in prison for making anti-war speeches.

In July 1917, the *Reichstag*, Germany's parliament, voted for a compromise peace, a proposal put forward by Erzberger, the future leader of the armistice delegation. But the *Reichstag* had no power over the German government and was ignored. When the British Labour Party called for a favourable response to the *Reichstag* Peace Resolution, the House of Commons voted heavily against it. And when socialists from Germany, Britain and France tried to meet for a peace conference in Stockholm, most were refused permission to travel by their governments.

These shops in the German capital, Berlin, have been looted by a hungry mob. Popular unrest made Germany's rulers fear there would be a revolution if they did not win the war quickly.

Siegfried Sassoon was a British poet who became an army officer and war hero, winning the Military Cross for valour. By 1917, however, he had become convinced that the war should be ended by negotiation. Risking court martial, he made a public appeal for peace:

'I believe that the war is being deliberately prolonged by those who have the power to end it. I am a soldier, convinced that I am acting on behalf of soldiers. I believe that this war, upon which I entered as a war of defence and liberation, has now become a war of aggression and conquest . . . I have seen and endured the suffering of the troops, and I can no longer be a party to prolong these sufferings for ends which I believe to be evil and unjust.'

Sassoon might have been imprisoned, but instead his protest was put down to shell shock, and he was sent to a military hospital. He eventually returned to the front.

Source: J. Stallworthy, *Wilfred Owen*

Emperor Charles came to the throne of Austria-Hungary in November 1916. He desperately wanted to end the war, which he correctly believed would lead to the break-up of his empire.

Empires and nationalists

Yet some rulers, such as the young Emperor Charles of Austria-Hungary and Tsar Nicholas II of Russia, would have been glad to make peace. They feared that the strain of war would destroy their empires. Russia, Austria-Hungary and Ottoman Turkey were especially under threat because they were multinational states, held together by a dynastic ruler. They were menaced not only by socialist revolution but also by nationalist movements.

In January 1917, the Allies declared themselves in favour of a degree of self-rule for some subject peoples of the Austro-Hungarian Empire – Poles, Czechs, Slovenes, Croats, Serbs and Romanians. President Wilson also adopted the principle of national 'self-determination'. With this encouragement, the various national groups increased their political agitation. There were outbreaks of mutiny by national minorities in the Austro-Hungarian army.

The Ottoman Empire was also threatened by nationalism, particularly by a British-backed Arab revolt that began in 1916. The Ottomans took brutal pre-emptive action against one prominent national group, the Armenians, several million of whom were exterminated in deportations provoked by their alleged support for Turkey's enemies.

Revolution in Russia

The first empire to crack under the strain of war was Russia, which had suffered a string of costly defeats since 1914. In March 1917, protests against bread shortages in Petrograd turned into a popular revolution. Tsar Nicholas II was forced to abdicate and a provisional government began to organize democratic elections. Through much of Russia, effective power was exercised by revolutionary councils of workers and soldiers – the soviets.

Russian Tsar Nicholas II and his family in exile in Siberia after the 1917 revolution. They were later shot by the Bolsheviks.

The provisional government continued to pursue the war, ordering an offensive in the summer of 1917 that ended in catastrophic defeat. The Russian army began to fall apart through mass desertions and indiscipline. Meanwhile, with the aid of Germany, an exiled revolutionary socialist, Vladimir Ilyich Lenin, returned to Petrograd and proclaimed a policy offering the Russian people 'Bread, Peace, and Land'. In November, Lenin's Bolsheviks seized power in the name of the soviets. Lenin immediately launched a ringing call for a general peace 'without annexations or indemnities'. On 15 December, an armistice was agreed between Russia and Germany.

Many Russian troops fought bravely in the failed offensive of the summer of 1917, but then the army quickly fell apart.

The weakness of the Bolshevik government allowed nationalists in Finland, Estonia, Lithuania, Latvia, Ukraine, Belarus, Moldova, Poland, Armenia,

Azerbaijan and Georgia to assert their independence. Germany backed these nationalists to achieve the dismemberment of the Russian Empire. On 3 March 1918, the Bolsheviks were forced to accept the humiliating peace treaty of Brest-Litovsk, which signed

The Bolshevik leader Vladimir Ilyich Lenin inspired many workers and soldiers with a belief that they could build a new world.

Lenin's peace appeal

On 8 November 1917, the day after the Bolshevik seizure of power in Russia, Lenin addressed representatives of soldiers, workers and peasants from throughout the Russian Empire. He read out a proclamation to 'the Peoples of All the Belligerent Nations', proposing a 'just and democratic peace' without annexations or indemnities. An American eyewitness, John Reed, described an overwhelming tide of emotion sweeping the hall as delegates believed the war was over at last.

Lenin did not expect governments to respond favourably to his appeal. He believed the war would turn into a world revolution as socialist workers of different nations stopped fighting one another and attacked their capitalist bosses instead.

away a large part of the former Russian Empire. The new would-be independent national states were immediately subject to close control and intense economic exploitation by Germany and Austria-Hungary.

No compromise

The first peace of the war had come through the victory of one side and the collapse of the other, with absolutely no compromise. It was increasingly clear that this would also happen on the Western Front. There was an outbreak of anti-war strikes in German factories in January 1918, but these were easily suppressed. With victory complete in the East, in March 1918 Germany's military leaders – Field Marshal Paul von Hindenburg and General Erich von Ludendorff – planned a last gamble on the Western Front, seeking total victory before US troops could enter the war in force. The Germans' spring offensive was to prove the decisive moment of the conflict and the beginning of the end of the war.

Russian revolutionaries, on the right of the table, are forced to accept humiliating peace terms at Brest-Litovsk. The Germans were merciless in victory.

From Armageddon to armistice

On 23 March 1918, Germany's ruler, Kaiser Wilhelm II, granted all German schoolchildren a 'victory day' holiday. It was two days since the German army had launched a great offensive – codenamed Operation Michael – on the Western Front. The offensive was intended to win the war, and initial results made the Kaiser confident that it would.

Through April and May, the German forces continued to press forward in fierce battles, edging towards Paris and vital Allied communication centres. The view of the war situation among British, French and American leaders was grim. At the start of June, the British even discussed the possibility of withdrawing their troops from France altogether, to prevent them being cut off and destroyed by the enemy advance.

Germany's ruler Kaiser Wilhelm II, the cousin of Britain's King George V, tied his personal prestige to the success of the March offensive. It was known as the Kaiserschlacht – the Emperor's Battle.

German troops attack French defensive positions during the 1918 spring offensive. It appeared to many soldiers at the time that the Germans were about to win the war.

Turn of the tide

But the Germans were suffering massive casualties: 348,000 men in the first six weeks of the spring offensive alone. In the early summer they were also struck by the beginning of the influenza epidemic, which disabled 500,000 of their men. Meanwhile, fresh US troops were arriving at the rate of 250,000 a month, rapidly replacing the casualties suffered by the Allies. In July, the German advance ground to a halt.

Wounded soldiers from both sides help one another through the streets of St Quentin. The German offensive ran out of steam as casualties mounted in the face of a determined fight-back by the Allies.

The following month, the Allies took the offensive. Massed British and French tanks led Australian and Canadian infantry into battle at Amiens, inflicting a heavy defeat on the German forces. Ludendorff called 8 August the 'black day of the German army'. The British in particular had by now become significantly technically superior to the Germans, inventing a new form of mobile warfare using tanks and aircraft. US troops were also bringing a fresh spirit to the front. In early September, under the command of General John Pershing, they inflicted a setback on the Germans at the St Mihiel salient. A notable feature of St Mihiel was the number of German troops who surrendered – more than 13,000. The German soldiers had been promised final victory in 1918. Disillusionment was the inevitable result of being thrown back once more on the defensive.

German soldiers retreat across the River Marne under fire in mid-July 1918. From this point onward, it was the Allies who took the offensive.

On 10 August 1918, Ludendorff gave Kaiser Wilhelm a gloomy account of the state of the German army on the Western Front. Summing up the situation, the Kaiser admitted:

'We have reached the limits of our strength. The war must be brought to an end.'

Source: A. Palmer, *Victory 1918*

A US soldier in action at the St Mihiel salient in September 1918. The Americans lacked battlefield experience, but fought with courage and determination.

Demoralization was as severe in the German high command as in the ranks. In early August 1918, Ludendorff and the Kaiser accepted that Germany could not win the war. During the following month, the situation of the Germans and their allies worsened rapidly. On 15 September, an Allied army based in Salonika, Greece, launched an offensive against Bulgaria. The Bulgarian forces put up little resistance and, two weeks later, Bulgaria surrendered. This left the way open for the Allied forces to attack Austria-Hungary from the south. At the same time, the Allies had launched another massive offensive on the Western Front.

The search for a ceasefire begins

On 29 September, Ludendorff told the Kaiser that Germany had to seek an immediate end to the fighting. As there were still no foreign troops on German soil, the German leaders hoped to win a deal that would leave their power and territory intact. They decided to ask President Wilson for a cease-fire, ignoring the French and British. To satisfy Wilson's desire for democracy, the Kaiser announced he was giving up his autocratic powers and accepting parliamentary government. He appointed a liberal-minded aristocrat, Prince Max von Baden, as chancellor (head of government).

Wilson wanted to play the role of peacemaker, and at first responded quite favourably to the German proposal for a ceasefire, to be followed by negotiations. But the British and French political and military leaders, and America's own military chiefs, soon persuaded Wilson that tough terms had to be imposed on Germany. Otherwise, the Germans might use a ceasefire as a chance to regroup their forces ready for a new war. On 20 October, the German government reluctantly accepted that there would have to be an armistice agreement with terms laid down by its enemies.

Empires fall

Austria-Hungary was even more desperate for peace than Germany. On 16 October, Emperor Charles tried to appease the United States by granting autonomy to national minorities. But it was too little, too late. Poles, Czechs

On 7 November 1918, four days before the armistice, a British army chaplain in the front line, Julian Bickersteth, wrote:

'The enemy is fighting a clever rearguard action and I do not see how we can hope to get him moving any faster . . . We all anticipate another six months of fighting at least.'

Source: N. Ferguson, *The Pity of War*

and other Slavs were by now fighting alongside the Allies for their freedom. President Wilson told the emperor that the subject nationalities could not now be denied full independence. By the time Austria-Hungary was granted an armistice on 3 November, the empire had virtually ceased to exist. The different national groups had effectively assumed power and were struggling to establish the borders of new independent states. Ottoman Turkey also surrendered at the end of October, leaving Germany as the only power still fighting the Allies.

In late October, as stubborn German troops on the Western Front continued to hold up the Allied offensive, German military leaders indulged fantasies of rejecting armistice terms and pursuing a policy of resistance to the death. But when Ludendorff and Hindenburg ordered all army commanders to fight to the finish, they were disowned by the Kaiser and Ludendorff was dismissed.

Germany's naval commander, Admiral Scheer, also opposed an armistice. On 28 October, he ordered the German fleet to sail into the North Sea for a final battle with the British navy. But the sailors refused to go. The north German port of Kiel was taken over by mutinous sailors and striking workers. Soon 11 major German cities were in the hands of revolutionary workers and servicemen. In Bavaria, in southern Germany, the left-wing politician Kurt Eisner set up a socialist republic.

End game

Meanwhile, at the end of October, the Allied Supreme War Council met to decide what armistice terms should be offered to Germany. They all accepted

A contemporary cartoon showing Marshal Foch, French Premier Georges Clemenceau, British Prime Minister David Lloyd George and US President Woodrow Wilson embarking on the 'Armistice Road'.

SOLDIER AND CIVILIAN.

MARSHAL FOCH (to Messrs. CLEMENCEAU, WILSON and LLOYD GEORGE). "IF YOU'RE GOING UP THAT ROAD, GENTLEMEN, LOOK OUT FOR BOOBY-TRAPS."

29

Wilson's 14 points as the basis for an armistice, but with a number of modifications. As the world's strongest naval power, Britain would not accept that there should be 'freedom of the seas' – at that very moment, the Royal Navy was blockading German ports. The French were insistent that Germany must be made to pay for the damage caused by the war, and this was accepted by the Americans. On 5 November, the Germans were told of the armistice terms and arrangements began for a German delegation to cross the battle lines.

Meanwhile, Germany was drifting out of the Kaiser's control as the power of revolutionary councils of workers and soldiers spread. The Kaiser wanted to use the army to crush the revolution by force, but Ludendorff's replacement, General Wilhelm Groener,

Friedrich Ebert, centre, the head of the new German Republic, was forced to rely on the army to keep him in power.

'No more loyalty'

By 8 November 1918, most German cities were in the hands of left-wing revolutionaries. Kaiser Wilhelm summoned the army chief, General Groener, and told him to send front-line troops to put down the revolution. But when Groener consulted other officers, he found that few believed their soldiers would obey an order to march on German cities. The following day Groener told the Kaiser bluntly: 'The army will march home in peace and order under its leaders, but not under the command of your majesty'. When one of the Kaiser's entourage insisted that the soldiers would stay loyal to their oath to obey their emperor, Groener told him: 'Today oaths of loyalty count for nothing'. The Kaiser's power was gone for ever.

told him it simply could not be done, because the soldiers would not obey orders. The leader of the Social Democrats, Friedrich Ebert, took over as head of government on 9 November and Germany was declared a republic. The Kaiser fled to exile in the Netherlands.

Surrender

The overthrow of the Kaiser took place while the German armistice delegation was in the Forest of Compiègne. They had arrived there on 8 November expecting to negotiate the best deal they could for their country. Instead, they were simply presented with terms which, they were told, must be accepted within three days. They sent the terms to Berlin for consideration. On the evening of 10 November, the reply came back from the German government and military leaders that the armistice was to be signed.

The terms of the armistice seemed harsh to the Germans. They were to withdraw their troops from all enemy territory they occupied. German territory on the west bank of the Rhine was to be occupied by Allied forces. The Germans were to hand over large quantities of military equipment, including most of their battle fleet. They were also at some future date to pay

The US commander General John Pershing believed the armistice had come too soon. He commented:

'What I dread is that Germany doesn't know that she is licked. Had they given us another week, we'd have taught them.'

Source: M. Gilbert, *A History of the Twentieth Century Volume 1: 1900–1933*

compensation for war damage. But most of Germany escaped military occupation by its enemies and the German army was allowed to march home from the front in good order. This would later allow many Germans to argue that they had never been militarily defeated.

General John Pershing commanded the US Expeditionary Force in France. He took a far more hostile stance towards the Germans than his political master, President Woodrow Wilson.

Building a new world

The armistice of 11 November 1918 silenced the guns on the Western Front, but much of Europe remained in turmoil. Many Europeans were menaced by hunger and disease following the disruption of war and revolution. The American Relief Association rushed in emergency food supplies to prevent people from starving.

The armistice did not even end the confrontation between the victorious powers and Germany. The British maintained a naval blockade of German ports and the armies stood ready to resume the war at any time. The failure to send the troops home caused much unrest among conscript soldiers eager to return to civilian life. There were mutinies by US and British Empire troops. Six Canadian soldiers at a camp in Wales were killed in the suppression of their mutiny.

The view of the defeat of Germany held by many people in the Allied countries was expressed in the inscription on the monument that was put up on the spot where the armistice was signed. The inscription read:

'Here on the 11 November 1918 succumbed the criminal pride of the German Reich . . . vanquished by the free peoples which it tried to enslave.'

Source: A. Bullock, *Hitler, a Study in Tyranny*

The winter of 1918–19 was a time of great hardship in Germany as, despite the armistice, the Allies kept up their naval blockade. Here, German women search for scraps of food in a daily struggle for survival.

The peace conference

Against this unsettled background, in 1919 the victors held a great peace conference in Paris. It was a worldwide event, with China, Japan, Siam (now Thailand) and 11 Latin American countries taking part, as well as the United States and European countries. There were, however, important absentees. Bolshevik Russia was not invited to send a representative. Nor were the defeated countries: Austria, Hungary, Bulgaria, Turkey and Germany. A German delegation was allowed to attend, but it was not to take part in any discussions or negotiations. Its role was simply to be told what peace terms the victors had decided to impose.

The peace conference was very poorly organized – a French diplomat, Paul Cambon, wrote that 'you cannot imagine the shambles, the chaos . . .' In practice, all major decisions were taken by British Prime Minister David Lloyd George, French Premier Georges Clemenceau and US President Woodrow Wilson, with Italian Prime Minister Vittorio Orlando included on issues that specifically concerned his country.

Wilson and Clemenceau, in particular, had very different attitudes to the problem of creating a peaceful future.

Lloyd George

Born in 1863, David Lloyd George was famous before World War I as a fiery Liberal politician who taxed the rich and challenged the power of the House of Lords. In 1916, he became prime minister at the head of a coalition cabinet, dedicated to winning the war at any cost. In November 1918, he won a general election during which the British public cheered the slogans 'Hang the Kaiser' and 'Make the Germans Pay'. But Lloyd George privately favoured a moderate peace, and did his best to soften French revenge on Germany. He was a keen supporter of the League of Nations and the rights of small nationalities.

Clemenceau

Georges Clemenceau was 76 years old when he was asked to become France's wartime prime minister in 1917. Known as 'the Tiger', he brought a passionate intensity to the business of winning the war. He had witnessed the humiliating defeat of France by Prussia in 1871, and felt both fear and hatred of the Germans. At the peace conference in 1919, he was determined to make it impossible for Germany to invade France again.

Clemenceau was obsessed with the need to weaken Germany and strengthen France. He saw this as the only way to avoid another invasion of his country by the Germans in the future. The idealistic President Wilson had little sympathy with this view. He wanted to create a new order that would settle Europe's problems justly once and for all. He believed that if nations were granted self-determination under democratic governments, they would have no more reason to attack one another. If any country returned to militarism and aggression, it would be stopped by the League of Nations, the international organization that Wilson planned to uphold the peace.

The Versailles Treaty

A whole series of peace treaties were concluded with the defeated countries: the Neuilly Treaty with Bulgaria, the Treaty of St Germain with Austria, the Trianon Treaty with Hungary, and the Treaty of Sèvres with Turkey. But it was the Versailles Treaty with Germany that was most crucial. Under the peace terms eventually presented

The 'big four' at the Paris peace conference. From left to right, British Prime Minister David Lloyd George, Italian Prime Minister Vittorio Orlando, French Premier Georges Clemenceau and US President Woodrow Wilson.

35

Article 231 of the Versailles Treaty stated that the war had been caused by *'the aggression of Germany and her allies'*, who were therefore responsible for *'causing all the loss and damage to which the Allied and Associated Powers and their nationals have been subjected'*. This article, known as the 'war guilt' clause, offended Germans more than any other aspect of the treaty.

Source: A. Sharp, *The Versailles Settlement: Peacemaking in Paris 1919*

to the Germans, Germany was to lose Alsace-Lorraine and a certain amount of other territory, and the Rhineland was to be occupied by Allied soldiers for 15 years. The German army was to be limited to 100,000 men, and they would have no tanks or aircraft. Germany was clearly stated to have been guilty of starting the war, and had to pay 'reparations' to France, Britain, Italy and Belgium to make up for the damage they had suffered. These reparations consisted of payments in kind — merchant ships and coal, for example — and money payments, the exact amount of which would be decided later.

Scuttling at Scapa Flow

At the end of the war, the 74 surface warships of the German High Seas Fleet were interned at the British naval base of Scapa Flow, in the Orkneys off north-east Scotland. On 21 June 1919 — the original deadline for Germany to accept the Versailles peace terms — German Admiral Ludwig von Reuter ordered his officers to sink their own ships, so that they could not be handed over to Britain. At noon, watched by a startled party of schoolchildren on an excursion, the great German fleet, including 15 of the largest battleships ever built, began to sink beneath the waves. The news of this defiant gesture was greeted with patriotic enthusiasm in Germany. It made Britain even more determined to force the Germans to sign the treaty.

A German warship, the Derfflinger, *disappears beneath the waves at Scapa Flow, sunk by its own crew in an act of defiance.*

When the peace terms were presented to the German delegation in May 1919, there was uproar in Germany. Most Germans did not feel their country was guilty of causing the war. Wilson's 14 points and his other statements had made them believe that they would be treated not as a defeated power to be punished, but on the basis of even-handed justice. The German government at first wanted to resume the war rather than accept the terms. But the German military leaders told the politicians that it was impossible for the army to resist the Allied forces. There was no alternative but to sign the treaty, which they reluctantly did on 28 June 1919.

A German representative signs the peace treaty in the Hall of Mirrors at the Palace of Versailles, watched by Wilson, Clemenceau and Lloyd George.

One eyewitness of the signing of the Versailles Treaty, US Secretary of State Robert Lansing, wrote:

'It was as if men were being called upon to sign their own death warrants. With pallid faces and trembling hands they wrote their names quickly and were then conducted back to their places.'

Source: P. Johnson, *A History of the Modern World*

Whether the peace terms imposed on Germany were unreasonably severe has been a subject of argument ever since. Many people in the victorious countries thought Germany had got off lightly. The British public, for example, had applauded calls for the Kaiser to be tried as a war criminal and hanged. Reparations, one of the most controversial parts of the treaty, were not a new idea. Germany had imposed heavy reparation payments on France after the Franco-Prussian War in 1871 – and the French had paid up. But, rightly or wrongly, the German people were united in their resentment of the Versailles Treaty, and as a consequence it was a direct cause of the outbreak of the next European war in 1939.

Europe in 1914

(Left and right) The collapse of Austria-Hungary, the defeat of Germany and revolution in Russia brought major changes to Europe's borders. As the Russian Empire changed into the Soviet Union, Poland, the Baltic states and Finland were able to assert their independence. Germany also lost territory to Poland. The Slav peoples of central Europe and the Balkans created the new states of Czechoslovakia and Yugoslavia. Austria, formerly the hub of a multinational empire, dwindled to a small landlocked state.

National boundaries

As well as being blamed for treating Germany too harshly, the peacemakers have often been criticized for the way the new borders of Europe were drawn. Instead of dividing the continent into clear-cut 'nation states', the peace settlement created new countries that contained a jumble of ethnic groups, some of them minorities that had no desire to be under their new rulers.

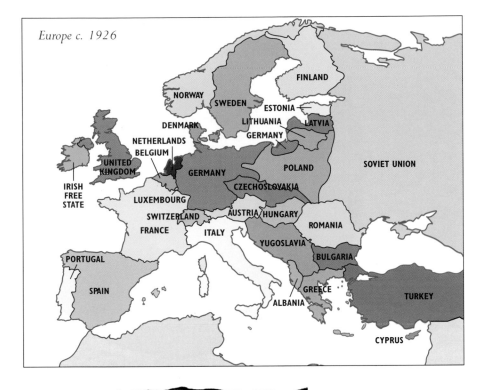

Europe c. 1926

The Russian civil war

By far the largest conflict in the aftermath of World War I was the Russian civil war. The 'White' armies, mostly headed by generals who had served under the Tsar, fought the 'Red' Army organized by the revolutionary Bolshevik government. Britain, France, the United States and Japan were among the countries that intervened in support of the Whites. Both sides in the civil war used extreme terror, including torture and massacre. By the time the Bolsheviks emerged victorious in 1921, the former Russian Empire was a wasteland. The disruption caused by the fighting led directly to the Volga famine of 1921–22, in which an estimated 3 million people died.

A Bolshevik poster urges workers to fight in defence of the revolution. Millions died in war, massacre and famine in the former Russian Empire in the four years after the end of the Great War.

But in practice, the Paris peacemakers had little control over what happened to the former territory of Austria-Hungary or the Russian Empire. The new states of Poland, Czechoslovakia, and Yugoslavia (the Kingdom of Serbs, Croats and Slovenes) were created by national leaders themselves. The borders of the new countries were largely decided by local wars – Hungary, for example, lost a large proportion of its territory after it was defeated by Czech and Romanian armies in 1919.

By far the heaviest fighting was in the former Russian Empire. The victorious powers intervened somewhat half-heartedly in Russia between 1918 and 1921, in support of Russians who wanted to overthrow Lenin's Bolshevik government. But the Bolsheviks won the civil war and succeeded in regaining control of much of the former Russian Empire. They lost a war with Poland in 1920, however, allowing the Poles to establish their border far to the east of the Curzon Line, set by the peacemakers as the eastern limit of Polish territory. Belarus and Ukraine were divided between Poland and Russia. Finland, Latvia, Lithuania and Estonia retained their independence.

The Paris peacemakers also failed to dictate what happened to Turkey. Under the terms of the Treaty of Sèvres, reluctantly signed by the government of the Ottoman sultan, Turkey was to lose not only its empire in the Middle East, but also a large part of its heartland in Anatolia. The lion's share would go to Greece. But, under the leadership of Kemal Atatürk, the Turks fought back against this plan to carve up their country. The

Mustafa Kemal, known as Atatürk (the father of the Turks), made Turkey a republic in 1923 and turned the country into a strong national state. He introduced the Roman alphabet in place of Arabic script and banned traditional Muslim dress.

triumph of Atatürk's army led to the expulsion of about a million Greeks from Turkey and the establishment of a Turkish Republic in 1923.

Imperial ambitions

Despite talk of 'self-determination', Europeans continued to dispose of peoples in the non-European world without asking their opinion or consent. Shantung, a part of China formerly controlled by Germany, was handed to Japan, despite the fact that China had supplied 100,000 labourers to work on the Western Front. Former German colonies in Africa and the Pacific were snapped up by Britain or its Dominions, under the guise of League of Nations' mandates. Indian soldiers had fought for their British rulers in large numbers, but India only received limited self-government in return, and was soon seething with agitation for independence.

The League of Nations

The one major triumph for President Wilson's idealistic approach to world affairs was that the Paris peace conference approved the League of Nations, the forerunner to the current United Nations. However, by the time the president went home to the United States, he was ill and facing a hostile Republican majority in Congress. Isolationist sentiment soared in the USA in the wake of the war. There was widespread hostility to any further entanglements in Europe. Congress failed to ratify the peace treaty, and the League of Nations came into existence in 1920 without the United States taking part. It was a bad omen for the future.

An artist's impression of an action during the war in which two Indian soldiers won the Victoria Cross. India felt it received little reward for having helped Britain defeat Germany.

Criticising the peace

One of the first people to attack the Versailles Treaty was the British economist John Maynard Keynes. His famous book, *The Economic Consequences of the Peace*, was published at the end of 1919. He argued that the demand for reparation payments from Germany was impractical and disastrous. He believed that instead the Germans should be given every help and encouragement to become prosperous again, since this would also bring prosperity to the rest of Europe. Keynes' book was very influential in the United States, where it helped turn people against the peace settlement.

John Maynard Keynes, seen here with his wife, was one of the most famous critics of the Versailles Treaty.

Winners and losers

In general, the peace conference did not lead to a Europe reflecting Wilson's ideal of self-determination. He had hoped that state borders would correspond to borders between areas inhabited by different nations. But the peoples of Europe were far too mixed up together to be easily separated in such a way. In any case, there were severe difficulties in applying the principle. Strictly applied, it would have left Germany a far larger country than before the war. To prevent this unacceptable result, German Austria was banned from uniting with Germany, and German minorities were left in many of the new countries around Germany's borders.

The new states of Czechoslovakia and the Kingdom of the Serbs, Croats and Slovenes (later called Yugoslavia) were not only based on an alliance between different nationalities, but also had large minorities that were not part of the ruling nations at all – for example, Bosnian Muslims in Yugoslavia and Sudeten Germans in Czechoslovakia. After its victory over Bolshevik Russia in 1920, Poland ended up with a population consisting of less than two thirds of ethnic Poles. The predominantly German-populated port of Danzig (Gdansk) was made a 'Free City' so that Poland could have access to the sea.

Hungary was one of the big losers in the peace settlement, giving up territory to Czechoslovakia, Yugoslavia and Romania. Italy and Yugoslavia struggled for control of the Croatian port of Fiume (Rijeka), which eventually went to the Italians in 1924.

The peace settlement gave Britain a mandate to rule Palestine, with the result that Britain became responsible for Jewish settlers such as these, building a new homeland.

The collapse of the Ottoman Empire at the end of World War I transformed the map of the Middle East. Turkey became a republic. France was given the League of Nations mandate to control Lebanon and Syria, while Britain was mandated to rule Palestine, Transjordan and Iraq. Hijaz and Yemen became independent kingdoms, though Hijaz was soon taken over by Najd to create Saudi Arabia.

During the war, Britain had promised Arabs in the Middle East that they would have their freedom when the Ottoman Empire was defeated. In the peace settlement, however, Britain and France divided the Middle East between them. Britain was given a mandate by the League of Nations to control Palestine, Jordan and Iraq, and France was mandated to control Syria and Lebanon. The Arabs were left with Arabia, although Arab princes were set up in Jordan and Iraq under overall British control. During the war, Britain had also promised the Jews a homeland in Palestine. The first Palestinian Arab protests against Jewish immigration occurred in 1920. Wartime promises to create an independent Armenian state in eastern Turkey were forgotten.

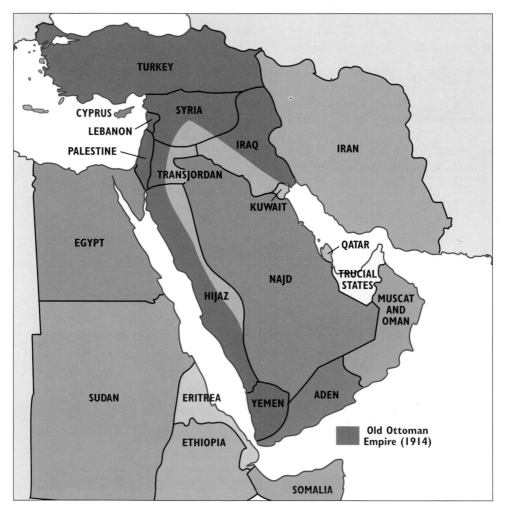

Old Ottoman Empire (1914)

From one war to the next

World War I was described by Allied political leaders as 'a war to end wars'. They hoped that the sacrifice of lives might be justified by the creation of a stable and lasting peace. But instead the Great War destabilized the world economy and the world's political systems. Tragically, it was destined to lead directly to another, even more destructive, world war 20 years later.

Counting the cost

Almost 9 million soldiers died in action in World War I. Millions more were permanently disabled. The overwhelming majority of those who died were young men. France lost one in ten of its entire male population. In Germany, among men who were aged between 19 and 22 when the war started, the death rate was one in three. The disruption of the war and its aftermath also created millions of refugees: Greeks fleeing Turkey, Turks fleeing Greece, Russians escaping from the revolution, Germans quitting territory handed to Poland. There were also millions of soldiers who had to re-adapt to civilian life, and for whom jobs needed to be found.

The war left hundreds of thousands of men severely disabled. These blinded German ex-servicemen are being trained to become fruit farmers.

There was relatively little physical destruction, compared with World War II. Even the war zone of north-eastern France was rapidly restored. British losses of merchant ships, sunk by U-boats, were quickly made up. But the general economic disruption was profound. Britain emerged from the war owing massive sums of money to the United States – these debts were still being paid off in the 1960s. Britain was, in turn, owed large sums by France and other wartime allies. Despite being one of the principal victors, Britain found it difficult to create a 'home fit for heroes' after the war. Mass unemeployment soon hit industrial areas of the country and did not go away again until World War II. In many other countries – for example, Italy and Hungary – economic disruption was more extreme.

A British poster underlines the fate of so many men who served their country in the war, but returned home to find there were no jobs to be had.

YESTERDAY-THE TRENCHES TO-DAY-UNEMPLOYED

Deaths in action in World War I	
Germany	1,800,000
Russian Empire	1,700,000
France	1,400,000
Austria-Hungary	1,300,000
Britain and its Empire	947,000
Italy	615,000
Romania	335,000
Turkey	325,000
Bulgaria	90,000
Serbia	55,000
United States	49,000
Total	**8,616,000**

Source: M. Gilbert, *A History of the Twentieth Century, Volume 1: 1900–1933*

Failure of democracy

At the end of the war, there seemed a possibility that left-wing revolutions, of the kind that had occurred in Russia in 1917, would take place in many countries. However, short-lived revolutionary governments in Hungary and Bavaria were soon defeated. In Berlin, an uprising by extreme left-wing Spartacists was crushed in January 1919 and its leaders, Karl Liebknecht and Rosa Luxembourg, were murdered. Even in the United States, the authorities cracked down hard on anarchist groups and left-wing trade unions.

But the defeat of left-wing revolutionaries did not guarantee the future of democracy, which soon began to collapse across Europe. In Italy, post-war discontent led to a takeover of power by Benito Mussolini's fascists. Mussolini crushed the socialists and communists and, in the course of the 1920s, turned Italy into a militaristic right-wing dictatorship. Other European countries in which democracy lost out to authoritarian or dictatorial regimes in the 1920s and 1930s included Spain, Portugal, Poland, Hungary, Romania, Austria and, most important of all, Germany.

German communist Rosa Luxemburg, murdered in Berlin in 1919 after leading an attempted revolutionary uprising.

The fascist leader Benito Mussolini (second from right) came to power in Italy in 1922 after staging a 'march on Rome'.

Mussolini

Before the Great War, Benito Mussolini was a well-known Italian socialist journalist. His experience of the war turned him into an extreme nationalist and militarist. He believed that war 'put the stamp of nobility on those nations that have the courage to face it'. In 1919, he formed the fascist movement in Italy. He used his black-shirted fighting squads, mostly former soldiers, to attack and intimidate his political opponents. After coming to power in 1922, he created a dictatorship that became a model for many other countries in Europe. A man of immense vanity, he eventually led Italy into a disastrous involvement in World War II. He was executed by Italian partisans in 1945.

Mussolini tried to project a tough image, wearing military uniform and adopting symbols of power such as the eagle.

Germany in chaos

Germany remained in upheaval for years after the war. The overthrow of the Kaiser led to the setting up of the democratic Weimar Republic in 1919. But the republic was threatened by violence from extremists both on the left and on the nationalist right. Right-wing nationalists denounced the Versailles Treaty as the source of all Germany's problems. They created the myth that the German army had not been beaten on the battlefield, but had instead been 'stabbed in the back' by socialists and Jews, who had agreed to humiliating peace terms and overthrown the Kaiser. (Jews were always hate figures for German nationalists.) Matthias Erzberger was assassinated by extremists in 1921, as a punishment for the crime of having led the armistice delegation.

Germany did everything in its power to avoid making reparation payments to the Allies. In 1923, the French and Belgians sent in troops to occupy the industrial Ruhr district of Germany, in order to enforce payment of reparations. The local population responded with strikes and passive resistance. The German government printed money recklessly, setting off hyper-inflation on a scale never seen before or since. By the summer of 1923, a meal in a German restaurant could cost 1,500 million Deutschmarks. By November, one US dollar was worth 4,200 billion Deutschmarks.

Perhaps surprisingly, German democracy survived this crisis. In Munich, Adolf Hitler, now a right-wing agitator, with the backing of Ludendorff, attempted to launch a coup to overthrow the regime, but failed ingloriously. Eventually a deal on reparations was agreed, French and Belgian troops were withdrawn, and during 1924 something like normal life resumed in Germany.

French troops occupy the Ruhr region of Germany in 1923.

A propaganda photo of the future German dictator Adolf Hitler in prison after the failed Munich coup of 1923. He was locked up for only nine months.

Crash and depression

Between 1925 and 1929, there was a period when it was possible to believe in the illusion of restored peace and prosperity. An economic boom in the United States helped a worldwide economic recovery. Germany joined the League of Nations in 1926 and two years later more than 60 countries signed the Kellogg–Briand Pact, renouncing war in the future.

But the economic recovery that underpinned this optimism was built on shaky foundations. In 1929, US stock market prices plummeted in the Great Crash. Facing financial ruin, American financiers withdrew their money from other countries, especially Germany, throwing them in turn into economic crisis. As mass unemployment ravaged the United States, trade throughout the world slumped. Banks collapsed in Austria and Germany. By 1932, one in four German workers was unemployed.

German soldiers keep watch over the Rhine after marching into the demilitarized Rhineland in the spring of 1936.

The rise of Hitler

Economic collapse led to political breakdown and a search for strong governments. In Germany, true democracy ceased in 1930, when the government took to ruling by emergency decree. Adolf Hitler, as leader of the Nazi Party, came to power in 1933, and quickly created a ruthless police state to support his dictatorship.

Hitler blamed Germany's hard times on the Versailles Treaty and the influence of the Jews. He combined measures to drive Jews out of German society with a relentless campaign to undo the Versailles settlement step by step. In 1933, he took Germany out of the League of Nations. In 1935, he formally announced that he was breaking the limits imposed by the Treaty on the size and armaments of the German armed forces. In 1936, his troops marched into the Rhineland, in defiance of the Treaty which had declared it a demilitarized zone. In March 1938 he annexed Austria, which had been expressly forbidden to unite with Germany by the Paris peacemakers. Later in the same year, he absorbed the Sudetenland area of Czechoslovakia, which had a primarily German population.

Hitler's troops marching through Vienna after the annexation of Austria.

Slide to war

By this time, the League of Nations had proved powerless to stop the rise of militarism worldwide. When the Japanese invaded Manchuria in 1931, Japan was criticized by the League, but no positive action was taken. In 1935, when Mussolini invaded Ethiopia, the League imposed economic sanctions on Italy, but to no effect. By 1937 Japan was engaged in a full-scale invasion of China, while Italy and Germany had sent troops to Spain to back the forces of General Franco in the Spanish Civil War. As a force for peacekeeping, the League of Nations was defunct.

In April 1939, justifying his actions in a speech addressed specifically to US President Franklin D. Roosevelt, Hitler expressed his hatred of the Versailles Treaty:

'I have . . . endeavoured to destroy sheet by sheet the treaty which in its 448 articles contains the vilest oppression which peoples and human beings have ever been expected to put up with.'

Source: J. Fest, *Hitler*

As Hitler unravelled the Versailles Treaty, the leaders of Britain and France, two of the very few democracies left in Europe, dithered. The only way they could stop Hitler was by starting a war, and this they did not want to do, partly because the tragic experience of World War I had made them fearful of another armed conflict.

Japanese officers in Manchuria. The Japanese invasion of Manchuria was condemned by the League of Nations, but to no effect.

A scene from the Spanish Civil War: both Italy and Germany sent forces to help General Francisco Franco to victory.

Hitler was also helped by the general acceptance of the principle of national self-determination at the end of the previous war. As he pressed to expand Germany's borders to include all German-speaking people, many thought he had right on his side.

In the spring of 1939, Germany destroyed Czechoslovakia. German troops occupied the Czech areas of Bohemia and Moravia. Slovakia became in theory independent, but in practice a German puppet state. Hungary also seized a slice of Czechoslovakia for itself. Hitler's next target was Poland. He demanded control of the port of Danzig. Britain and France committed themselves to fighting if Poland was attacked. On 1 September 1939, German troops crossed the Polish border. As a consequence, Britain and France declared war on Germany.

Germany's revenge

In 1940 Hitler succeeded in doing what the Germans had failed to do in 1914: he conquered France. On 21 June 1940, on exactly the same spot where the German delegation had signed the armistice of 11 November 1918, a French delegation was forced to sign an armistice imposed by Germany. Adolf Hitler even had the railway carriage in which the 1918 armistice had been signed brought from a museum in Paris to the Forest of Compiègne for the occasion. Hitler sat in the same seat that Marshal Foch had occupied in 1918, as one of his generals read out a statement to the French delegation. It referred to the 'dishonour and humiliation' of the German people that had begun in that place, and declared that 'the profoundest disgrace of all times' was being wiped out. The German revenge for the armistice of 1918 was complete.

Germany invaded Poland in September 1939, starting World War II in Europe. About one in five Polish citizens was to die in the course of the war.

In essence, the war of 1939–45 was a continuation of the war of 1914–18. The Allies in World War I had imposed a victors' peace on Germany, but had then lacked the will to uphold its terms. The United States had tried to create an idealistic peace based on democracy and freedom, but had then withdrawn into isolation and failed to resist the rise of new militarist regimes. When Hitler defeated France in the summer of 1940 and drove British forces out of continental Europe, he saw it as a triumphant revenge for the German catastrophe of 1918. But he was eventually to lead his country to an even greater disaster in 1945.

Remembrance

World War I had a different impact on different countries. For the defeated powers, especially Germany, the memory of the war was a source of bitterness. In the 1920s, remembering those who had fallen in battle was often an occasion for political demonstrations demanding revenge against those held responsible for the defeat. In Russia, the revolution of 1917 was endlessly commemorated, but the war that had brought the revolution about was largely forgotten. Americans had a tendency to turn their backs on the war, which most soon came to regard as a mistake they did not want to repeat in the future.

But in Britain and France, from the end of the war onward, people were determined that the sacrifice made by the soldiers of the Great War should not be forgotten. War memorials inscribed with the names of the dead were put up in most towns and villages. In many schools, brass plaques listed former pupils who had lost their lives. On the first anniversary of the armistice, it was decided to observe two minutes' silence at 11.00 a.m. throughout Britain and its Empire. All work stopped. Cars, buses, trams and trains halted. Conversations were interrupted in mid-sentence. People stood stock still in the street or in their houses. For many years, the silence was observed with the same intensity on each Armistice Day. Britain erected a Cenotaph (meaning 'empty tomb') in Whitehall, designed by the architect Sir Edward Lutyens, which became the focus for a remembrance ceremony every year from 1920. The wearing of artificial red poppies began the following year.

A service of remembrance at the Menin Gate war memorial, Ypres, in 1928. The memorial is engraved with the names of 55,000 dead British soldiers.

The Cenotaph in Whitehall, central London, has been the focus of Remembrance Day in Britain since 1920. This ceremony was photographed in 1929.

Burying the dead

All countries faced the problem of attempting to give a decent burial to those who had died in battle. Over half those who had died either were never found or could not be identified. France's largest Great War monument, the ossuary of Verdun, holds the bones of 130,000 French and German soldiers. Most of the German and Austrian dead ended up in mass graves on foreign soil, but walls of remembrance were erected in both countries as a focus for grieving. Most of the American dead were shipped home for burial in the United States.

The Unknown Soldier

After the Great War, there was a strong feeling in all combatant countries that the contribution of ordinary soldiers, sailors and airmen should be recognized, rather than that of generals or political leaders. On Armistice Day 1920, Britain held a state funeral for an Unknown Warrior, who represented all those who had lost their lives in the war. The body of a dead serviceman was selected at random, brought back by warship from France, and buried with great ceremony in Westminster Abbey. The French held a similar ceremony on the same day at the Arc de Triomphe in Paris. The following year, an American serviceman was buried as the Unknown Soldier in Arlington National Cemetery, Washington, DC.

The American tomb of the Unknown Soldier in Washington, DC. It carries the inscription: 'Here Rests in Honored Glory an American Soldier Known But to God'.

The British, however, decided to bury their men where they had fallen, creating a string of military cemeteries across north-eastern France. Wherever possible, the British dead were buried in individual graves. If the body could not be identified, the headstone bore an inscription written by the poet Rudyard Kipling: 'A Soldier of the Great War Known Unto God'. Great monuments were erected at the Menin Gate and Thiepval, bearing the names of tens of thousands of the fallen. The Imperial War Graves Commission (now the Commonwealth War Graves Commission) took on the task of creating these cemeteries and maintaining them up to the present day.

Images of war

The official view of the war – shared by a large number of ordinary people, including many who had fought in the front line – was that it had been a tragic experience, but one also steeped with heroism and a sense of noble duty fulfilled. In Britain, for example, Lloyd George had spoken of 'Honour, Duty, Patriotism and . . . Sacrifice' as 'the great everlasting things that matter for a nation'. This view did not exclude a recognition of the horrors suffered by the men at the front, but saw the suffering as justified by a high purpose.

Even in the victorious nations, however, disillusionment soon became the dominant note in the years after the war. Soldiers who returned from the war to unemployment and poverty, for example, were bound to ask what the sacrifice had been for. In 1921, the British Armistice Day ceremonies were disrupted by unemployed ex-soldiers with placards reading: 'The dead are remembered, we are forgotten'.

Unwanted men

In all countries, many soldiers returning from the war felt they received little in return for their sacrifice. Leslie Langille, a young American from Chicago, wrote ironically that 'a grateful government gives us an honourable discharge from the army – and sixty dollars … just about enough money to buy a suit of civilian clothes'. The fate of many soldiers was unemployment. As Langille cynically put it: 'Another and different kind of battle faces us. How about a job?'

In the years following the Great War many ex-servicemen were forced to beg or provide street entertainment to earn money.

Many ex-soldiers came to look back with nostalgia on the comradeship of the trenches. In all combatant countries, there were large war veterans' associations that helped men keep up the bonds they had formed during the conflict. Some of these war veterans' groups became centres of nationalism and militarism. But more were devoted to the avoidance of future war and the memory of the fallen.

The growth of pacifism

By the late 1920s and early 1930s, a wave of anti-war feeling had begun to change the way the Great War was seen. Instead of an example of heroic sacrifice, the war was represented as futile slaughter. Heroism and patriotism were widely condemned as lies that had led millions to their deaths. The work of British anti-war poets such as Wilfred Owen and Siegfried Sassoon became well-known. When the anti-war novel *All Quiet on the Western Front (Im Westen Nichts Neues)* by German author Erich Remarque was published in 1929, it sold 2.5 million copies in its first 18 months.

Canadian veterans receive awards for valour in 1998, 80 years after their great but costly victory at Vimy Ridge.

The militaristic dictators of the 1930s, such as Adolf Hitler (who banned *All Quiet on the Western Front*), tried to promote fighting spirit and a warlike attitude far more extreme even than that prevailing before the Great War. But when war broke out again in 1939 there were no cheering crowds in the streets of Berlin, Paris or London, as there had been in 1914. No amount of propaganda could erase the lesson that had been learned.

Student pacifism

In February 1933, the Oxford Union, the student debating society of Oxford University, voted overwhelmingly in favour of the proposal that 'this House will not fight for King and Country'. The vote was inspired by revulsion at the patriotic enthusiasm that had led to mass slaughter during the Great War. It caused a sensation not only in Britain but around the world, because Oxford students were an élite in Britain and were the sort of people who would be expected to form the officer class in time of war. However, in 1939, they fought unhesitatingly.

In 1968, a Great War veteran, C.E. Crutchley, wrote:

'Remembrance Day, if it is to serve the purpose for which it was created, must act as a warning – as well as a reminder of men's past deeds of shame.'

Source: H. Cecil and P. Liddle (eds), *Out of Control: At the Eleventh Hour*

Sanctuary Wood, one of the Great War cemeteries of northern France and Belgium that are still well tended and much visited today.

The Great War today

Anti-war feeling tended for many years to undermine respect for the remembrance associated with Armistice Day. Many people felt that the official ceremonies glorified war. During the 1960s and 1970s, it seemed that the Remembrance Day observances might die out. Yet the tragedy of 1914–18 continued to maintain a grip on the popular imagination. Towards the end of the twentieth century, as the very last survivors of the Great War were dying, interest in Remembrance Day actually revived. The war memorials still stood, the war graves were still tended and visited. There was no sign that the Great War would be forgotten.

Lines from Laurence Binyon's poem, 'For the Fallen', written in 1914, are recited every year on Britain's Remembrance Day:

'They shall grow not old, as we that are left grow old:
Age shall not weary them, nor the years condemn.
At the going down of the sun and in the morning
We will remember them.'

Date list

1914

August — The major powers of Europe go to war.

1915

7 May — A German U-boat sinks the liner Lusitania, provoking anti-German riots in Britain.

1916

5 June — Arabs revolt against the Ottoman Empire.

7 November — Woodrow Wilson is elected US President.

1917

15 March — Tsar Nicholas II of Russia abdicates.

6 April — President Wilson declares war on Germany.

2 November — Britain says it favours the creation of a homeland for Jewish people in Palestine. This is called the Balfour Declaration, after British foreign secretary A. J. Balfour.

7 November — The Bolsheviks, led by Lenin, seize power in Russia.

15 December — Russia and the Central Powers sign an armistice.

1918

8 January — President Wilson proposes his 14 points as the basis for an end to the war.

3 March — The treaty of Brest-Litovsk, imposed by Germany on Bolshevik Russia, deprives Russia of vast areas of eastern Europe.

21 March — A massive German spring offensive on the Western Front drives the Allies back towards Paris.

18 July — Allies embark on a counter-offensive.

8 August — Allied forces launch a successful offensive at Amiens.

29 September — Germany's military leaders say their government must seek an immediate armistice.

30 September — Bulgaria surrenders to the Allies and signs an armistice.

16 October — Austria-Hungary grants self-rule to its national groups.

28 October — German sailors mutiny in the port of Kiel. This triggers a revolutionary uprising throughout Germany.

30 October — The Allies sign an armistice with Turkey. Czech nationalists in Prague declare an independent state of Czechoslovakia, breaking away from Austria-Hungary.

2 November — Hungary declares itself an independent republic.

3 November — Austria-Hungary, which has already virtually ceased to exist, signs an armistice with the Allies.

9 November — Germany is proclaimed a republic and Kaiser Wilhelm flees to the Netherlands.

| 11 November | Germany signs an armistice with the Western Allies. Jozef Pilsudski becomes leader of an independent Polish republic. |
| 4 December | Nationalists create the Kingdom of the Serbs, Croats and Slovenes, later known as Yugoslavia. |

1919

18 January	The Paris Peace Conference opens.
21 June	The German fleet is scuttled at Scapa Flow.
28 June	German representatives sign the Versailles Treaty.
11 November	The first two-minutes silence in memory of the war dead observed in Britain.

1920

10 January	The League of Nations comes into existence, without the United States taking part.
10 August	The Treaty of Sèvres between Ottoman Turkey and the Allies gives Greece a large part of Anatolia.
11 November	Burial of the Unknown Soldier in Britain and France.

1921

| 18 March | The Treaty of Riga makes peace between Bolshevik Russia and Poland. |

1922

| 31 October | Fascist leader Benito Mussolini becomes head of government in Italy. |

1923

11 January	French and Belgian troops occupy the German Ruhr.
29 October	Turkey officially becomes a republic, with Kemal Atatürk as its first president.
8 November	An attempted coup by Adolf Hitler in Munich fails.

1928

| 27 August | The Kellogg–Briand Pact, renouncing war, is signed by 65 states. |

1929

| October | The Wall Street Crash ends the economic boom in the United States, starting the era of the Great Depression. |

1933

| 30 January | Adolf Hitler becomes German chancellor, dedicated to the complete overthrow of the Versailles Treaty. |

1938

| 13 March | Germany takes over Austria in the Anschluss. |
| 30 September | Czechoslovakia is forced to hand the Sudetenland region to Germany after the Munich Conference. |

1939

| 15 March | Czechoslovakia ceases to exist after German troops march into Prague. |
| 1 September | German troops invade Poland, beginning World War II. |

1940

| 21 June | France signs an armistice imposed by the victorious Germans. |

Glossary

annexation one country taking over part or all of the territory of another country.

armistice an agreement between two sides in a war to stop fighting so that they can negotiate a peace treaty.

Austria-Hungary created in 1867, the Dual Monarchy of Austria-Hungary was ruled by the Habsburg emperors Francis Joseph (to 1916) and Charles (1916–18). The Austrian half of the Dual Monarchy was dominated by Germans and the Hungarian half by Hungarians, but many other nationalities lived there, including Czechs, Poles, Croats, Slovenes and Serbs.

autonomy a degree of self-government falling short of full independence.

Bolsheviks a Russian political party led by Vladimir Ilyich Lenin and dedicated to communist revolution. The Bolsheviks seized power in Russia in November 1917 and eventually created the Soviet Union.

cede to give up rights to or possession of (a country or region).

Dominion one of the self-governing countries of the British Empire. The Dominions were Australia, New Zealand, South Africa and Canada.

dynastic ruler an emperor or monarch who rules by right of birth.

hyper-inflation a rapid rise in prices that makes money almost worthless.

indemnity compensation for loss or damage – in this context, the demand by the winning side that the losers pay the cost of the war.

isolationism a movement of opinion in the United States against American involvement in European or world affairs.

League of Nations mandate a system of disguised colonialism, under which countries such as Britain and France were allowed to rule territories in Asia, Africa and the Pacific as 'trustees' authorized by the League of Nations.

militarism an active preference for the use of armed force and war, rather than peaceful methods.

multinational state a country containing people of different ethnic groups speaking different languages, held together by obedience to a central government or ruler, rather than by a shared national identity.

oath of loyalty a solemn promise to obey and support a leader or state.

Ottoman Empire a Turkish-ruled empire that, in 1914, controlled much of the Middle East as well as the present-day area of Turkey.

reparations payments demanded of a defeated country by the victors to compensate for damage they have suffered in a war.

salient a point at which your own defensive line stuck out into enemy territory.

self-determination the principle that people should be ruled by a government of their choice, especially one that represents their own ethnic or national group.

socialism the belief that wealth should be equally shared by everyone and that large factories and businesses should not be owned by rich individuals. Some socialists believed in the revolutionary overthrow of existing society, while others, known as social democrats, believed in gradual change through parliamentary democracy.

Resources

Books to read

The best short book on the Great War is still British historian A.J.P. Taylor's *The First World War*, first published in 1963. It is quirky, often funny, always lively, and illustrated with a remarkable selection of photos. A longer, and more up-to-date, account of the war is military historian John Keegan's *The First World War*, published in 1998. Both Taylor and Keegan cover the armistice and its aftermath.

Some of the books written in the 1920s and 1930s by people who had experienced the war at first hand are still readily available in bookshops or libraries. They include Siegfried Sassoon's *Memoirs of an Infantry Officer; Goodbye to All That* by Robert Graves; Vera Brittain's *Testament of Youth;* and Erich Remarque's novel *All Quiet on the Western Front*. These were the books that fixed the image of the war as a senseless slaughter.

In the 1990s, there has been a spate of best-selling novels about the war, notably Pat Barker's trilogy *Regeneration*, *The Eye in the Door* and *The Ghost Road*, and Sebastian Faulks' *Birdsong*. A very interesting book that might be slightly more difficult to find is *The Missing of the Somme* by Geoff Dyer. This is an account of a journey to the World War I cemeteries by a group of irreverent young people, reflecting on the nature of the war and what it can still mean to us today.

Other recommended activities and resources

If there is a war memorial in your area, have a closer look at it. You might reflect on how the people who put up the memorial wanted the war remembered – have they emphasized courage and military valour, or suffering and loss? If you ever have a chance, a visit to the war cemeteries and former battlefields in northern France is an impressive experience. The Imperial War Museum in London has fascinating exhibits on the war.

Sources

Gordon Brook-Shepherd, *November 1918: The Last Act of the Great War*. Collins, 1981.

Allan Bullock, *Hitler, a Study in Tyranny*. Penguin, 1990.

Hugh Cecil and Peter Liddle (eds), *Out of Control: At the Eleventh Hour*. Leo Cooper, 1998.

Geoff Dyer, *The Missing of the Somme*. Hamish Hamilton, 1994.

Niall Ferguson, *The Pity of War*. Penguin, 1998.

Joachim Fest, *Hitler*. Weidenfeld & Nicolson, 1974.

Martin Gilbert, *A History of the Twentieth Century, Volume 1: 1900–1933*. HarperCollins, 1997.

Paul Johnson, *A History of the Modern World*. Weidenfeld & Nicolson, 1983.

John Keegan, *The First World War*. Hutchinson, 1998.

Alan Palmer, *Victory 1918*. Weidenfeld & Nicolson, 1998.

Alan Sharp, *The Versailles Settlement: Peacemaking in Paris 1919*. Macmillan, 1991.

Jon Stallworthy, *Wilfred Owen*. Oxford University Press and Chatto & Windus, 1975.

John Stevenson, *The Penguin Social History of Britain: British Society 1914-45*. Penguin, 1984.

A.J.P. Taylor, *The First World War*. Penguin, 1966.

Peter Vansittart (ed.) *Voices from the Great War*. Jonathan Cape, 1981.

Index

If a number is in **bold** type, there is an illustration.